Tittenhurst Park

A Pictorial History

Tittenhurst Park

A Pictorial History

Copyright 2017
by The Cardinals

All Rights Reserved. No part of this publication may be reproduced, stored in a retrieval system, or transmitted in any form or by any means, electronic, email, photocopying, recording, scanning, or otherwise, without the prior written permission of the Publisher. The content of this book is of a historical, educational, and newsworthy nature, and is made available in the name of the public interest. Considering the purpose and character of the transformative use of the text, photos and illustrations in creating a new work, the Publisher is confident that their use does not directly affect and/or compete with any potential claimant's business or potential for income. The Publishers are confident that there is no part of this book that is in violation of, or infringes upon, anyone's copyrights, trademarks, licensing, privacy, or postmortem publicity rights.

Limit of Liability/Disclaimer of Warranty: While the Publishers and the Author(s) have used their best efforts in preparing this book, they make no representations or warranties with respect to the accuracy or completeness of the contents of this book and specifically disclaim any implied warranties of merchantability or fitness for a particular purpose. Neither the Publisher nor the Author(s) shall be liable for any loss of profit or any other commercial damages, including, but not limited to, special, incidental, consequential, or other damages.

All reasonable effort has been made to contact the photographers and copyright owners of all images printed in this publication. Any omissions or errors are inadvertent and will be corrected in subsequent editions, provided written notification is sent to the Publisher. Many of the images in this book are transformative works and are protected by their own copyrights as well as the overall copyright protecting the contents of this book.

Campfire Publishing/Campfire Entertainment Network publishes its books in a variety of formats. Some content that appears in print may not be available in electronic books, and vice versa. The content of this book was generated during scholarly research on architectural history.

For information on any books published by the Campfire Entertainment Network, or for bulk & wholesale orders, or to schedule interviews with any of the Authors, please contact Cardinal@CampfireNetwork.com.

Acknowledgments & Dedication

It affords us great and sincere pleasure to acknowledge, and express our sincere gratitude to John Bezzini, D.C. Blackbird, Peter Blakey, Pattie Boyd, Shelley Germeaux, David Goddard, Lawrence Gowan, Ron Kelly, Jonas Herbsman, Simon Hilton. Sean Jackson, Neil Kernon, Neil Murray, Chris O'Dell, Barbara O'Donnell, Mike O'Donnell, Dan Richter, Sara Schmidt, Debs Skeldon, Keith Smart, David Tickle, Keith Robinson, Jack Perry, Steve Silberberg, Nigel Street, and Eddie Veale for their generous assistance in our research. A special thanks goes to Gerhard Bohrer & Servi Stevens for their friendship and their many priceless observations, which can not be too highly emphasized and are always appreciated. Despite all the contributions made from so many people, from so many sources, the responsibility for any errors, omissions, misinterpretations, or shortcomings anywhere in this book remain ours alone.

Dedicated to:
Radar
(1998 - 2016)

Imagine you are home. You have the entire day to yourself. You can do anything. You can go anywhere. Then you get hit with a great idea. You slowly walk into your bedroom and see that none of the cats are in there. They are all on the other side of the house, or on the porch. You have the room all to yourself. So you lay down on your back and you close your eyes. And you think to yourself: Radar-Radar-Radar. You then whisper the words "Radar-Radar-Radar." Slowly. Quietly. So low that you could barely be heard a few feet away. You then keep thinking: Radar-Radar-Radar. In less than a minute you hear low thumping sounds in the hallway. Boompa-Boompa-Boompa. You hear the sound getting closer. A moment later the sound has entered the room. You hear a grunt and then the sound of movement on the bed. You feel the mattress go down ever so slightly. You then feel 1 paw, then 2, then 3, then 4 on your stomach and chest. You then feel warm air on your neck. You open your eyes and you see Radar looking right at you. How did he know you were there? Did he hear you calling for him in your mind? Did he hear the whispers of his name from across the entire house? It doesn't matter. He then licks your face with his scratchy tongue. It makes you laugh. You put your hands on his sides and pull yourself back a bit, just out of reach of his scratchy tongue, and you two look into each other's eyes. That, dear reader, is priceless. That is love. That is friendship. So please go to your local kill shelter and bring home a new friend, and give him or her your love and friendship, and you'll get some in return. I promise. Because I know. I miss Radar's love and friendship every single day. He came from a shelter. He was the best.

Contents

Introduction

Early History & Maps
19th Century Residents
20th Century Residents
Exterior of the House
Grounds & Gardens
Trees & Flowers
Cottages
Sgt Pepper Caravan
Interior of House
Ascot Sound Studios
Imagine
Startling Studios
Ring O' Records
The Sheikh
Tittenhurst Today

Introduction

Despite the fact that it has always been a private residence and has not been open to the public since the mid 20th-century, Tittenhurst Park is one of the most famous country homes outside of London. The reason why is that John Lennon called it his home from the Spring of 1969 until the end of the Summer of 1971. As a result, the general public was able to see brief glimpses of the estate in photos of The Beatles that were taken in August, 1969. Though perhaps even better known is the promotional film for his well-known song "Imagine" that was filmed in the "white room" in the manor house.

Surprisingly, though John Lennon was once one of the most photographed men in history, there are not many photos available of him at his life at Tittenhurst Park. Those that are available can rarely be used due to copyright issues.

As with the case of the Dakota apartment building in New York City, there is so much more to know than that Tittenhurst Park was where John Lennon lived. The estate has an astounding history, the gardens have always been astonishing, and the architecture of the assorted structures on the property have always been of great interest.

This pictorial history has been put together to celebrate all that most people do not know about this legendary estate known as Tittenhurst Park.

A Pictorial History

Early History & Maps

Tittenhurst Park is a Grade II listed early Georgian country house in an estate of over 70+ acres (29+ hectares) off London Road at Beggar's Bush near Ascot and over the parish border into Sunningdale, both in the English county of Berkshire.*

The present house dates back to 1737, although the facade is largely circa 1830. In 1869, the property was owned by Thomas Holloway, philanthropist and founder of two large institutions which he built nearby known then as: Holloway Sanatorium, and Royal Holloway College. Upon his death he bequeathed his entire estate to his sister-in-law who continued living there with her husband George Martin. Tittenhurst Park was next owned by Thomas Hermann Lowinsky, the former general manager of the Hyderabad (Deccan) Co coal mines in India. Lowinsky was interested in the gardens and built up an outstanding collection of rhododendrons, winning a gold medal for them from the Royal Horticultural Society. The flower 'Mrs Tom Lowinsky' was named by him to honor his wife. Though they were both born in India, Lowinsky's children grew up at Tittenhurst Park. His daughter, Xenia Noelle Field, became a well-known author, prison reformer and horticulturist. His son Thomas Esmond Lowinsky was known for painting portraits and fantasy scenes.

A Pictorial History

Sunningdale is a large village and civil parish in the Royal Borough of Windsor and Maidenhead in Berkshire, England. Sunningdale is located close to the present border with Surrey, and is not far from Ascot, Sunninghill and Virginia Water. It is situated 24 miles (38 km) west of Central London and 7 miles (11 km) northeast of Camberley on the A30 old trunk road. Sunningdale has a railway station on the Waterloo to Reading line which has the only level crossing on the entire length of the A30.

Tittenhurst Park

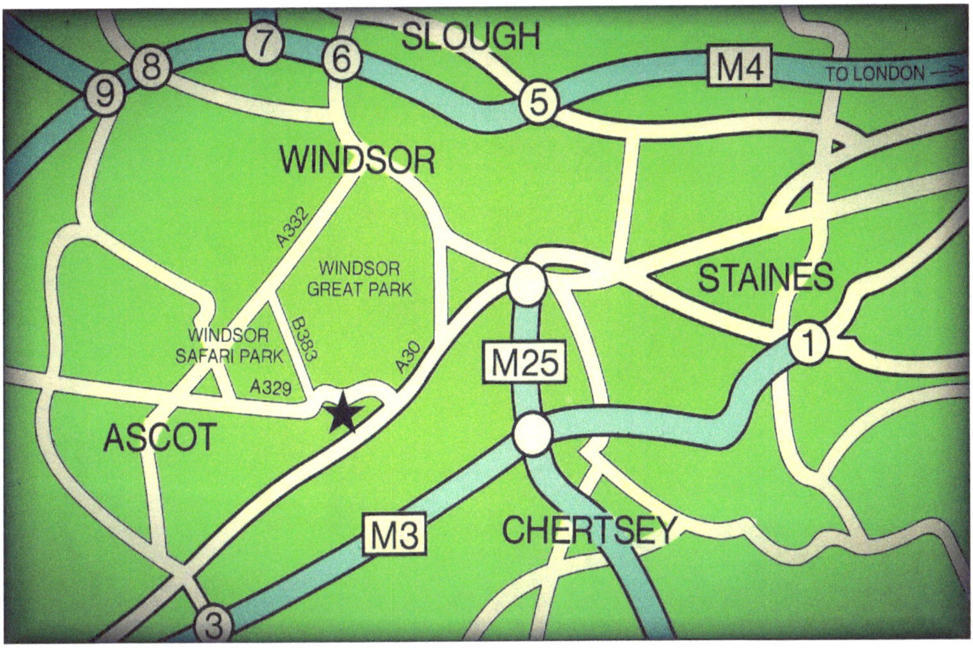

The present-day civil parish of Sunningdale came into existence in 1894 under the provisions of the Local Government Act 1894; the village had previously been part of Old Windsor.

A Pictorial History

19th Century Residents

Thomas Holloway

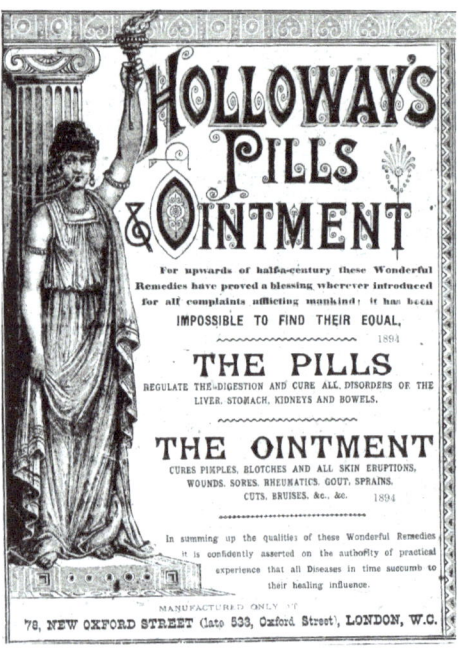 

Thomas Holloway (Sept. 22, 1800 – Dec. 26, 1883) was an English patent medicine vendor and philanthropist. Holloway had business connections with an Italian, Felix Albinolo, who manufactured and sold a general purpose ointment. This gave Holloway the idea to set up a similar business himself in 1837. He began by using his mother's pots and pans to manufacture his ointment in the family kitchen. Seeing the potential in patent medicines, Holloway soon added pills to his range of products. Holloway's business was extremely successful. A key factor in his enormous success in business was advertising, in which Holloway had great faith. Holloway's first newspaper announcements appeared in 1837, and by 1842 his yearly expenses for publicity had reached over £5,000 (GBP). By the time of his death, he was spending over £50,000 a year on advertising his products. The sales of his products made Holloway a multi-millionaire, and one of the richest men in Britain at the time.

Holloway's products were said to be able to cure a whole host of ailments, though scientific evaluation of them after his death showed that few of them contained any ingredients which would be considered to be of significant medicinal value.

Holloway had become extremely wealthy by the late 1860s and bought Tittenhurst Park. He lived there with his wife. Her sister, Sarah Anne Driver, also lived there with her husband George Martin, as did Holloway's sister Matilda. Jane died in 1875, aged 61; Holloway died there on 26 December 1883, aged 83.

A Pictorial History

Holloway Sanatorium was an institution for the treatment of the insane on 22 acres of parkland near Virginia Water, Surrey, England within the boundary of Egham and today's contiguous London urban area, about 22 miles south-west of Charing Cross. It was designed in an elaborate Franco-Gothic style by W. H. Crossland, and built between 1873 and 1885. The Sanatorium was officially opened by the Prince and Princess of Wales (later King Edward VII and Queen Alexandra) in 1885. The Illustrated London News reported, "the building containing about 600 rooms, disposed on four floors, and capable of accommodating about 250 patients. The expense hitherto incurred is about £300,000.

Tittenhurst Park

Royal Holloway College was founded in 1879. It was officially opened in 1886 by Queen Victoria as an all-women college. It became a member of the University of London in 1900. In 1945, the college admitted male postgraduate students, and in 1965, around 100 of the first male undergraduates. In 1985, Royal Holloway merged with Bedford College (another former all-women's college in London). The merged college was named Royal Holloway and Bedford New College (RHBNC), this remaining the official registered name of the college by Act of Parliament. The campus is dominated by the Founder's Building, a Grade I listed red-brick building modelled on the Château de Chambord in the Loire Valley, France.

A Pictorial History

20th Century Residents

The Lowinskys

About 1898, the house was purchased by Thomas Hermann Lowinsky, the former general manager of the Hyderabad (Deccan) Co. coal mines in India. He was an active member of the Royal Horticultural Society and won their gold medal for his rhododendrons, an outstanding collection of which he built up at Tittenhurst, including one he named 'Mrs Tom Lowinsky'. Amongst Lowinsky's children who grew up at the park was his daughter, Xenia Noelle Field, the prison reformer and horticulturist.

Thomas Lowinsky (son)

Xenia Lowinsky (daughter)

The Mosenthals

(left)
John Singer Sargent
1856 - 1925
MRS. GEORGE MOSENTHAL
signed John S. Sargent, u.l., and dated 1906, u.r.
oil on canvas
36 by 28 3/4 in.
(91.4 by 73 cm)

In 1906. Sargent completed Marguerite Mosenthal's portrait. Her husband George was one of four brothers who oversaw a vast mercantile empire in South Africa. From their headquarters in Port Elizabeth, the Mosenthal family began their business in the 1830s. Their chain of small country stores, which supplied items such as drapery, hosiery, and hardware to the rural communities along the Eastern Cape, quickly grew into the largest merchant house in South Africa. Though the Mosenthal's vast fortune was established in trade. They were also active in the nascent diamond business. By the end of the nineteenth century, the Mosenthal's were powerful "Randlords" - those entrepreneurs who controlled the early diamond mining industry in South Africa.

(left)
Caricature Portrait of Mrs. George Mosenthal
inscription: u.l., graphite: Mrs. Mosenthal by J. S. Sargent
Graphite on heavy off-white wove paper (menu)
Dec. 31, 1907
17.8 x 11.4 cm (7 x 4 1/2 in.)

A Pictorial History

Peter Cadbury

Peter Egbert Cadbury (6 Feb. 6, 1918 – April 17, 2006) was a British entrepreneur. His father was a World War I flying ace and managing director of Cadbury Brothers, the chocolate enterprise. Cadbury never worked in the family business. He followed his father into flying, with an early career as a test pilot for jet fighters. He qualified as a barrister, playing a minor role in the Nuremberg War Crimes trials, before deciding his future did not lie in law. Borrowing £75,000 from his father, Cadbury purchased the Keith Prowse theatre booking agency. After this, he was involved as a company director in the establishment of Tyne Tees Television and led the consortium responsible for Westward Television, the first ITV franchise holder for the southwest of England, becoming its Executive Director. He also owned his own airline and travel business.

Tittenhurst Park

Cadbury's country estate was Tittenhurst Park at Sunninghill in Berkshire. He was an animal lover who kept a parrot, a Great Dane, and a Rwandan gorilla. He was married three times. The first time was to Benedicta Bruce in 1947 (with legendary Spitfire pilot Douglas Bader as best man), with whom he had a son and a daughter; the marriage ended in divorce in 1968. He married again in 1970 to Mrs. Jennifer Morgan-Jones, who was 27 years younger than he, and with whom he had another son (Joel Cadbury, one-time owner of the Groucho Club), before they divorced in 1976. In that same year, he married a third time, to Mrs Jane Mead, with whom he had two more sons. Cadbury died on April 17, 2006, at the age of 88.

Tittenhurst Park

In one of the most favoured residential districts in the Home Counties.

A CHARMING AND WELL-APPOINTED GEORGIAN HOUSE.

of moderate size with compact accommodation on two floors.

7 principal bedrooms and 4 bathrooms. Entrance and staircase halls. 3 beautifully proportioned reception rooms. Well appointed kitchen. Two self-contained staff flats.

Oil-fired central heating and all main services.

Garage 4/5 cars. Stabling. Entrance Lodge.

Magnificent gardens and grounds of international repute with a unique collection of rare trees and shrubs. Wide spreading lawns, etc. Hard Tennis Court. HEATED SWIMMING POOL. In all **about 21 ACRES.**

Additional land and cottages available if required.

FOR SALE FREEHOLD.

John & Yoko

John Winston Ono Lennon, MBE (born John Winston Lennon; 9 October 1940 – 8 December 1980) was an English singer and songwriter who co-founded the Beatles, the most commercially successful band in the history of popular music. (Dan Richter collection)

Tittenhurst Park

(left) View of John & Yoko seated in the dining room. The bay windows behind them are large enough to be opened as doors to allow access to the yard. (Dan Richter collection)

John Lennon spent twice the purchase price on renovations, transforming the interior of the house to saitisfy how he and Yoko would like it. Among other things, they commissioned a set of hand-woven Oriental rugs, and had a man-made lake built (without planning permission) which they could see from their bedroom window. During 1970 and 1971, John & Yoko began to visit the United States, first for Primal Therapy at Dr. Arthur Janov's Primal Institute in California, then for child custody hearings over Ono's daughter Kyoko Chan Cox, in Houston and New York City. Because Yoko Ono had spent her late teens and her twenties living in Manhattan, and felt more at home there than in London, she gave John a grand tour to show him all that New York City had to offer them. On August 31, 1971 John & Yoko left Tittenhurst Park and moved to New York City permanently.

A Pictorial History

Daniel Richter (born 1939 in Darien, Connecticut) is an American mime and actor. He is remembered as playing the leader of a tribe of ape-men in 2001: A Space Odyssey. Richter went on to work and live with John Lennon and Yoko Ono, directing the photography of their 1972 Imagine video at Tittenhurst Park. He has written a memoir of his experiences with Lennon and Ono, "The Dream is Over," which was released in 2012. (Dan Richter collection)

(below, left) Dan Richter throws a bone in honor of Arthur Clarke at Olduvai Gorge November 19, 2000. (below left photo: Will Richter - Shadow Greg Cummings,; "Moon-Watcher" in 2001: A Space Odyssey) (below, right) Dan, John, and Yoko having dinner with their attorney before the "kidnapping" in Palma. (Dan Richter collection)

Tittenhurst Park

As a good friend of Yoko Ono, Dan was trusted to personally assist her and John Lennon in personal and business matters. Among his responsibilities was to assist in the creation of the UK's first professional home recording studio, ordering furniture and other items for the house, and overseeing a series of creative projects, including photography and cinematic endeavors shot on the estate. (Dan Richter collection)

(right) While working with John & Yoko, Dan and his wife and child lived in one of the guest cottages on the property.. John gave them an assortment of unusual clothing that he had acquired from the closing of the Apple Boutique, including flaboyant shirts and a jacket that was made especially for him by The Fool.* (Dan Richter collection)

A Pictorial History

Ringo Starr

Deciding to stay long-term in the United States, Lennon sold Tittenhurst Park to his former bandmate Ringo Starr, who purchased the property on September 18, 1973.

Richard Starkey, MBE (born 7 July 1940), known professionally as Ringo Starr, is an English musician, singer, songwriter and actor who gained worldwide fame as the drummer for the Beatles.

On January 20, 1965, Starr proposed marriage to his girlfriend Maureen Cox at the Ad-Lib Club, above the Prince Charles Theatre, London.

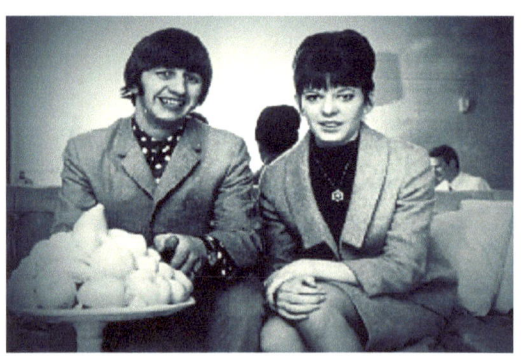

Tittenhurst Park

(left) Ringo Starr and his wife Maureen bought their first home together soon after their marriage. Sunny Heights was a large mock Tudor house in Weybridge, Surrey, less than a mile from John Lennon's house Kenwood.

(right) Ringo bought Sunny Heights for £50,000 and later bought a 16th-century mansion named Brookfield, in Elstead, from Peter Sellers.

(left) Ringo sold Brookfield to Stephen Stills. On April 25, 1969, Ringo and his family then moved into Roundhill, on Compton Avenue, Highgate, London

A Pictorial History

(left) Barbara Bach (born Barbara Goldbach; August 27, 1947) is an American actress and model who played the Bond girl Anya Amasova in the James Bond film The Spy Who Loved Me (1977) as well as the spy Maritza Petrovi in Force 10 from Navarone (1978).

Bach met Ringo Starr on the set of the film Caveman in February, 1980. They were married on April 27, 1981, a few weeks after the film's release.

(right) Caveman is a 1981 American slapstick comedy film written and directed by Carl Gottlieb and starring Ringo Starr, Dennis Quaid, Shelley Long and Barbara Bach.

(above) View of the east side of the manor house, showing the windows of the master bedroom upstairs and the "white room." The stone steps lead down from the upper plateau to the east gardens. The majestic lifesize lion statues were brought to Tittenhurst by Ringo. (right) View of southeast side of house, with a pair of antique planters, a wood bench, and lion statues in the foreground.

A Pictorial History

Exterior of House

(above) View of the north facade of the manor house c. 1960s. The center door leads to the original entry to the home. On the top floor, on the left, is a window to the master bedroom. In the center is the window for the en suite bathroom. On the right is another bedroom that John & Yoko used as a closet for their clothes. On the bottom right is the window to the room that John & Yoko had painted completely white. On the right is the library, where some residents kept a billiard table.

Tittenhurst Park

(above) View of the north entry of the manor house c. 1970s. The windows to the side of the table allow light to enter the large entryway. The transom window above had the words THIS IS NOT HERE etched into it soon after John & Yoko made Tittenhurst Park their home. The statuary was brought over from Kenwood by Lennon. They were moved around to various locations around the house and were left by Lennon when he moved to New York City in 1973.

A Pictorial History

(above) View of the east side of the manor house c. 1960s as seen from the lower terrace of the grounds and gardens. This image, taken in the summer or spring, shows the beauty of the evergreen trees and brilliant red flowers in bloom.

(above) View of the northeast side of the manor house c. 1960s as seen from the lower terrace of the grounds and gardens. In the foreground is a vintage stone retaining wall, topped with ornate stone urns and some over-flowing evergreens. On the lawn is a contained flower bed containing an antique planter in the center. In the distance can be seen stone urns & planters. The north side of the house can be seen on the right side of this photo, partially obscured by large evergreen hedges to the side of the circular driveway. (colorized version from the Cardinal collection)

A Pictorial History

(above) View of the terrace from the top floor bedrooms, overlooking the gardens on the eastern and southern portions of the property. At the far end is a beautiful handcrafted and hand painted octagonal-shaped wooden dovecot surrounded by trees and flowers in an assortment of pots. The railing runs long the entire perimeter. Also on the terrace is a heavy set of cast iron lawn furnture, including chairs, settee, and table in a grape pattern. (colorized version from the Cardinal collection)

(above) View of the east side of the manor house as seen from behind the staue of Diana, located on a large foundation in the center of a pond, surrounded by garden urns filled with flowers. By the time this photo was taken grass has covered the former gravel-covered path.. This statue is perfectly appropriate considering that In Roman mythology, Diana was the goddess of the hunt, the moon, and nature being associated with wild animals and woodland, and having the power to talk to and control animals. (Dan Richter collection)

Grounds & Gardens

(above) View of the Staue of Diana in the center of the pond, surrounded by decorative urns filled with flowers. A gravel path encircles it, with stone pedestals and planters at the perimeter, and at the crossways of the gravel paths. In the distance can be seen a classic concrete rounded balustrade railing. (colorized version from the Cardinal collection)

(opposite, right) View of man standing next to the 90+ ft. tall Incense Cedar tree, located to the south of the statue of Diana. (colorized version from the Cardinal collection)

A Pictorial History

Tittenhurst Park

(above) Eastern view of the formal Long Walk c. 1906, with the Diana Statue seen in the distance. (colorized version from the Cardinal collection)

(opposite, left) View of the Incense Cedar, decorative urn, and gardens c. 1904, along the Lower Terrace in the east gardens. (colorized version from the Cardinal collection)

A Pictorial History

(above) View of the formal flower garden along the Long Walk with evergreen hedges arranged in swirl designs. (colorized version from the Cardinal collection)

(above) Evergreen hedges contain blooming flowers along a gravel path, c. 1907. (colorized version from the Cardinal collection)

Tittenhurst Park

(above) View of flower garden with decorative antique planters, urns, statues, and hedges, c. early 1900s. (colorized version from the Cardinal collection)

(opposite, left) View of the east side of the manor house as seen from behind the extensive branches of the Blue Atlas Cedar circa 1964. Cedrus atlantica, the Atlas cedar, is a cedar native to the Atlas Mountains of Morocco (Middle Atlas, High Atlas), to the Rif, and to the Tell Atlas in Algeria. (colorized version from the Cardinal collection)

(above) Northern portion of the Long Walk, c. 1960s.

(above) View of the gardens as seen from the east side of the house. In the distance can be seen the T-Rex statue brought to the gardens by Ringo circa 1970s. (Peter Blakey collection)

(above) View of path and stone steps along a southern slope in the gardens c. early 1900s. (colorized version from the Cardinal collection)

(above) The border of the property c. 1970 with wildflowers growing along an expanse of lawn to the edge of an evergreen privacy hedge. (Dan Richter collection)

(above) Close-up view of "Daisy," the life-size Tyrannosaurus rex sculpture, soon after it was placed in the gardens. It was built off-site and assembled on the property where it remained for roughly 15 years.

(opposite, right) View of the T-Rex in the gardens c. 1980s. (Peter Blakey collection).

(above) View from behind the Tyrannosaurus rex statue with the manor house seen in the distance. (Neil Murray collection)

A Pictorial History

In 1970 John & Yoko installed a man-made lake that they could see from their bedroom window. It was located roughly 500 ft from the manor house. In the center was an island with a pavillion. The bottom of the lake was lined with thick rubber that periodically filled with air bubbles that needed periodic maintance. (below, Peter Blakey collection).

Tittenhurst Park

In the 1990s the Sheikh had at least two different lake houses built along the southern perimeter of the body of water. The 50+ ft. tall Black Oak tree can be seen in the foreground. (DavidGoddard.org collection)

"It looks like it has been there for ever, but it has got a rubber bottom."
— John Lennon

(right) View from above the lake & lake house, circa 2017. Koi carp were deliberately introduced into the habitat to keep the spread of water-borne larvae and the level of plant growth under control.

A Pictorial History

At the bottom of the slope on the south side of the manor house was a swimming pool that offered beautiful views of surrounding landscape. Along the side was added a small dressing room. In the above this is a diving board and slide. In the below photo the slide was removed and the patio area was expanded. (Peter Blakey collection)

(above) View of the swimming pool c. 1960s from above the slope, looking southward with a grand view of the landscape.

Trees & Flowers

Tittenhurst Park

HERBACEOUS CALCEOLARIAS

A Pictorial History

Tittenhurst Park

(above) 50+ ft. tall Araucaria araucana (commonly called the monkey puzzle tree, monkey tail tree, Chilean pine, or pehuén) is an evergreen tree growing to 3–5 ft in diameter and 100–130 ft in height. It is native to central and southern Chile and western Argentina. Tittenhurst Park had a male and female monkey puzzle tree growing next to one another. (right) Golden-headed Yew. (colorized versions from the Cardinal collection)

(opposite, left) This Weeping Blue Atlas cedar or "cedrus atlantica pendula" was photographed by the eminent dendrologist A. F. Mitchell in 1963.

A Pictorial History

Tittenhurst Park

(left) View of the gardens along the southern portion of the porch below the terrace on the east side of the house.

(below) View of the Sophora japonica, commonly called Japanese pagoda tree or Chinese scholar tree, is native to China and Korea, but not Japan. It is a medium to large deciduous tree that typically matures to 50-75' (less frequently to 100') tall with a broad rounded crown. It is generally cultivated for its attractive compound foliage and fragrant late summer flowers.

(opposite, left) Sequoiadendron giganteum (giant sequoia; also known as giant redwood, Sierra redwood, Sierran redwood, Wellingtonia or simply Big Tree. The ones at Tittenhurst are referred to as the pendulum or "weeping" variety.

Cottages

To the southwest of the manor house was a structure built in the Cape-Dutch style. It was sometimes referred to as the "Assembly Hall" until Lennon allowed Srila Prabhupada, the founder of the Hare Krishna movement, and over a dozen of his devotees, to stay in some of the guest cottages at Tittenhurst Park. Following that, the structure was referred to as the "Temple". Three or four times a week, the Swami, who later became known to the world as Srila Prabhupada, gave public lectures in the building, near a small Deity altar and a podium for Srila Prabhupada. Cape Dutch architecture is a traditional Afrikaner architectural style found mostly in the Western Cape of South Africa. The style was prominent in the early days (17th century) of the Cape Colony, and the name derives from the fact that the initial settlers of the Cape were primarily Dutch. The style has roots in medieval Netherlands, Germany, France and Indonesia. (photo circa early 20th century)

Tittenhurst Park

(above) View of the Cape-Dutch cottage from the east, showing a gravel path and evergreen bushes (Peter Blakey collection)

(right) The band Stormer poses in front of the entry to the Cape-Dutch cottage where The Beatles had posed during their last photo shoot. The band stands in front of a larger-than-life cut-out of musician, singer & poet Marc Bolan playing guitar and Ringo Starr (Ron Kelly collection)

A Pictorial History

(above) The Keeper's Lodge located on the northeastern side of the estate, with its own approach driveway off of London Road. The above photo, c. 1970s, shows the Sgt. Pepper Caravan parked on the lawn in front of the building.

(left) Vintage photo of the Keeper's Lodge from the southwest. Mock Tudor architecture first manifested itself in domestic architecture in the mid-to-late 19th century based on a revival of aspects of Tudor architecture & the style of architecture of the Middle Ages.

Tittenhurst Park

(above) At the time that this photo was taken c. 1980, Lennon's caravan was completely dilapidated and much of the paintwork had been worn off. To the side of the Caravan was a fire pit with stump seats around its perimeter. (Ron Kelly collection)

(right) Vintage photo of the Keeper's Lodge from the southeast. In the foreground can be seen when the stone retaining wall and wooden benches had seen better days. (colorized version from the Cardinal collection)

A Pictorial History

(left) View of the back of the Terrace Cottages. They are also known as the Forge Cottages because the building was once a part of the workshops to the west, where blacksmiths once lived and worked. Each apartment included a living area and kitchen downstairs, and a bathroom and bedroom upstairs.

(right) View of the front of the Forge Cottages circa 1970. The windows are to the kitchens. To the right are the backs of the garages, stables, and storage rooms. In the distance is a stone wall with a wooden fence door that once led to the Smithy. (Dan Richter collection)

Tittenhurst Park

(above) View of the garden buildings, stables, and tunnels for agricultural productions. On the upper left is London Road. Behind the trees is Whitmore Lane. (below) portion of the stables. (Peter Blakey collection)

A Pictorial History

Sgt. Pepper Caravan

In 1967 John Lennon purchased a caravan for his son Julian's 4th birthday. Before delivery to their home in Weybridge, Surrey, Lennon commissioned for it to be painted with a psychedelic design, and decorated and painted in bright colors with gilded accents, resembling that of his Rolls Royce. Yellow, red, and blue paint to create the Sgt Pepper motif and Romany art designs. The Showman, also known as a Burton caravan, was the type typically owned by circus and carnival travelers who wanted self contained accommodations while in transit. Such a caravan allowed space for a hand crafted bed, bespoke kitchenette, and even a wood burning stove. Most had two windows on each side, and even skylights for extra light. The Caravan was traditionally horse-drawn, but when Lennon wanted it transported to the island that he owned off the coast in Ireland it was simply hooked up to the back of an automobile.

Tittenhurst Park

(above & below) After having the caravan cleaned up, Ringo parked it to the side of the swimming pool. (Peter Blakey collection)

"During the making of Sergeant Pepper John decided to have the Rolls-Royce painted. Colour and design were of the utmost priority and he employed a firm of barge and caravan designers to do it for him. The idea came to him when he bought an old gypsy caravan for the garden." - Cynthia Lennon, from her book, "A Twist of Lennon"

A Pictorial History

Interior of House

(above) Early 20th century photo of the entry way on the north side of the house. The hall is clearly large enough to be used as a reception area, filled with large and comfortable furnishings. To the right is a staircase with wood balusters that leads on the first platform to the hall of the southern wing of the house. Turning left, and walking further, the stairs lead to the bedrooms directly above. In the background is the dining room with large windows overlooking the grounds and gardens. (colorized version from the Cardinal collection)

(above) Early 20th century of the dining room. The bay window on the far side of the room overlooks the southern portion of the property. (colorized version from the Cardinal collection)

(above) Early 20th century of one of the bedrooms, fully-carpeted, decorated in the Art Deco style that was trendy at the time. The custom-made bed of inlaid wood sits atop a low platform with elegantly-designed, brushed-silver railings. The comfortable-looking ottoman matches the shape & materials of the bed. There is a lacquered desk, gilded vanity table, upholstered vanity stool, a pair of tall mirrors, and a fine French Giltwood Bergère. The enclosed upholstered armchair has an upholstered back and armrests on upholstered frames. The bay windows with soft drapery overlook the gardens. (colorized version from the Cardinal collection)

(above) Another view of the bedroom shown on the previous page. Within the alcove are heavy curtains that frame velvet wallpaper with Art Deco metallic motifs.

(above) View of John & Yoko's bedroom c. 1970. In the forground is a TV atop an ornate rug. To the right is an ornate fireplace surround and mantel. The mattess sits atop a box spring on the floor. Behind the bed is the southernmost bay window with vertically-hinged natural-colored, wood shutters that fold into the wall.

(right) View of John & Yoko's en suite bathroom, including the round, jacuzzi-style, bathtub.

Tittenhurst Park

While Tittenhurst Park was leased out to musicians the original dining room was converted into a game room with a Snooker Table, Foosball Table, Pinball Machine, and other games. The fireplace and furnishings were provided courtesy of Ringo's company that he co-owned with Robin Cruickshank. The table in the above photo was listed for sale in 2015 for $600-$800.

(right) Whitesnake hanging out between recording sessions at Startling Studios. (photo to the right courtesy of Neil Murray)

A Pictorial History

(above) View of the master bedroom c. late 1970s. At this point Ringo Starr owned the property and he had the large room John & Yoko had created back to two bedrooms as it had been previously. The bedroom was completely carpeted. The folding shutters remained, but drapes were added to the sides. Behind the dresser and mirror is the window that overlooks the terrace.

Tittenhurst Park

(above) View of the 2nd master bedroom c. late 1970s. This one includes the en suite bathroom. The bay window overlooks the eastern gardens. The window on the left faces north and overlooks the driveway.

(above) View of the kitchen c. 1975. Though Ringo owned the property at this point, the kitchen still looked the same as it had when John & Yoko had lived in the manor house years earlier, with the stainless steel counters and appliances, the flagstone tile they had installed, and even the refectory table which was large enough to easily accomodate over a dozen people at once.

Tittenhurst Park

(above) View of the southeast side of the kitchen c. 1975, showing the circular staircase Lennon had installed that led to a film editing suite upstairs. In the corner is John Lennon's Wurlitzer jukebox. The door to the left leads to the dining room. The window overlooks the south lawn.

Ascot Sound Studios

> "John had just purchased a new home and asked me if I would like to build a studio within it, to save him from the commute into London. There was no real brief. He just said, 'Build me a studio as good as Apple'." - Eddie Veale

(above) The studio at Tittenhurst Park was the model that spawned a generation of home facilities, changing the face of studio recording. Up until that point, home studios had been no more than a room with a Revox machine and a microphone, more a place for the musician to trial ideas before getting into the proper studio. The Ascot project would be a first not only for Veale but also for the UK.

A few days later, Veale, going it alone under his new guise of Audiotek, met Lennon at Tittenhurst and together they selected a single-storey extension next to the kitchen but away from the main living areas as the ideal location. Construction began in August 1970, and for Veale it was to be his first solo construction project. There was a lot to learn, not least how to keep the rainwater out.*

Tittenhurst Park

(above) View of the custom console made for John Lennon by Dave Dearden, the founder of Audient. The original studio specified and constructed by Veale was eight-track, largely because the master machine was a 3M eight-track sent over from Apple who were moving to 16-track. The short lead time – Lennon wanted to start recording by Christmas 1970 – meant that there could be no pause for a bespoke console so the ever-resourceful Veale ended up building one from scratch.

"Consoles were all built to order at the time and the only serious console builder for studios was Cadac, but we didn't have time to wait for them," explains Veale. "We ended up using Cadac modules and we did the metalwork and the wiring. I had to corner-mount the monitor loud speakers to fit the available space. The speakers were based on my design for the Apple Studios, they were wedge shaped, using Altec drivers, and were placed above the window. I acquired a bit of a reputation for designing loudspeaker systems after that, and have enjoyed improving many studio control rooms over the years!"

The console (pictured) had 16 microphone input channels and four echo returns, eight master outputs, two foldback and two echo (reverberation) outputs. Monitor power amplifiers were Amcron, headphone and the other amplifiers were Quad. There were two EMT140 echo plates and an echo chamber. Microphones were Neumann and AKG. Stereo machines for mixdown and ADT were Studer B62.*

With the studio up and running on time, despite the presence of an increasingly impatient Lennon who was keen to start work before testing was complete, by the end of July 1971 most of the tracks for Imagine were recorded, and producer Phil Spector was literally in the mix.

"Having designed the place I took on the role of studio engineer for the album," says Veale, "so that I was on hand to deal with any problems as they arose. I worked closely with a couple of engineers from EMI, which was a huge learning curve for me and helped enormously when I came to design the home studio for George Harrison later on. By the time we were halfway through Imagine we had ironed out most of the wrinkles. It turned out to be quite an engineering achievement on all fronts – technical, soundproofing and isolation – not to mention the construction work. Even more learning on the job came when Spector called for Automatic Double Tracking for a vocal part*

> "I had no experience of ADT so I didn't have a clue how to get it right. In the end I drove to Abbey Road with Lennon, Phil Spector and a trail of engineers to create it there. As soon as I heard what they were after I realized what the problem was. The playback was reverse phase so what was coming back was out of phase. It took about five minutes to correct and then we had our own ADT effect at Ascot." - Eddie Veale

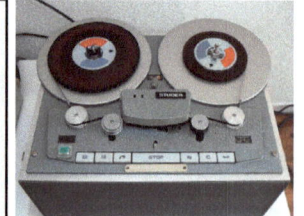

*History of Ascot Sound Studios text provided courtesy of Debs Skeldon.

Tittenhurst Park

A Pictorial History

Imagine

Imagine is the second studio album by John Lennon. Recorded and released in 1971, the album is the most popular of his solo works and the title track is considered one of Lennon's most popular songs. In 2012, Imagine was voted 80th on Rolling Stone magazine's list of the "500 Greatest Albums of All Time".

John Lennon – vocals, acoustic and electric guitars, piano; whistling on "Jealous Guy"; harmonica on "Oh Yoko"
George Harrison – electric and slide guitar on "I Don't Want to Be a Soldier", "Gimme Some Truth," "Oh My Love," and "How Do You Sleep?"; dobro on "Crippled Inside"
Nicky Hopkins – piano; electric piano on "Jealous Guy", "Oh My Love" and "How Do You Sleep?"; tack piano on "Crippled Inside"
Klaus Voormann – bass; upright bass on "Crippled Inside"
Alan White – drums on "Imagine", "Gimme Some Truth", "Oh My Love", "How Do You Sleep?", "How?", and "Oh Yoko!"; Tibetan cymbals on "Oh My Love"; vibraphone on "Jealous Guy"
Jim Keltner – drums on "Crippled Inside," "Jealous Guy," and "I Don't Want to Be a Soldier"
Jim Gordon – drums on "It's So Hard"
King Curtis – saxophone on "It's So Hard" and "I Don't Want to Be a Soldier"
John Barham – harmonium on "Jealous Guy"; vibraphone on "How?"
Joey Molland and Tom Evans – acoustic guitars on "Jealous Guy" (incorrectly credited as "I Don't Want to Be a Soldier")
John Tout - piano on "Crippled Inside" (incorrectly credited as playing "acoustic guitar")[40]
Ted Turner – acoustic guitars on "Crippled Inside"
Rod Linton – acoustic guitar on "Crippled Inside", "Gimme Some Truth" and "Oh Yoko!"
Andy Davis – acoustic guitar on "Gimme Some Truth", "How?" and "Oh Yoko!"
Mike Pinder – tambourine on "I Don't Want to Be a Soldier"
Steve Brendell – upright bass on "Crippled Inside"; maracas on "I Don't Want to Be a Soldier"
Phil Spector – harmony vocal on "Oh Yoko!"
The Flux Fiddlers (members of the New York Philharmonic) – orchestral strings.

Tittenhurst Park

Advertisement for Imagine from Billboard, 18 September 1971.

Startling Studios

Upon purchasing the estate Ringo Starr renamed the studio "Startling Studios." For the first couple of years it was used as his own personal studio. Beginning in 1975, he made the facility available for use by other recording artists. A promotional brochure was put together and sent to music labels and others in the music industry to stimulate interest in all the benefits and amenities Tittenhurst Park had to offer them.

> STARTLING STUDIOS IS A VERY SURPRISING PLACE.
> BECAUSE HERE IS AN EXCELLENT, WELL EQUIPPED COMMERCIAL STUDIO SET RIGHT IN THE HEART OF A BEAUTIFUL 72 ACRE BOTANICAL GARDEN LESS THAN ONE HOUR FROM LONDON. FAR ENOUGH FOR BANDS AND ARTISTS TO 'GET AWAY FROM IT ALL'. YET STILL REMAIN WITHIN EASY REACH. BUT THE SURPRISE DOESN'T END THERE. STARTLING STUDIOS IS ALSO A FINE COUNTRY HOUSE WITH WINDING STAIRCASES, GRACIOUS ROOMS AND AN AIR OF GOOD LIVING.

Tittenhurst Park

THE CONTROL ROOM AND STUDIO
THE STUDIO IS DESIGNED AND EQUIPPED TO INTERNATIONALLY ACCEPTED STANDARDS COMPLETE WITH 110 AND 240 VOLT SUPPLIES. FACILITIES PROVIDED INCLUDE A YAMAHA GRAND PIANO, HAMMOND C3 ORGAN WITH LESLIE FENDER RHODES 88 STEREO ELECTRIC PIANO, AND AN ARP 2500 SYNTHESIZER. THE MICROPHONES ARE BY NEUMANN, AKG, BEYER, SHURE, SENHEISSER AND ELECTROVOICE.

A Pictorial History

Tittenhurst Park

The 32 in, 32 out control room

Control room facilities are of an extremely high standard.
The desk is the highly versatile 32 in, 32 out MCI desk with quad capability.
The comprehensive range of auxiliary units includes:

16 and 24 track 2″ mastering machine. 3M 4″ track machine. Two B62 stereo mastering machines. Eventide digital delay.
Eventide digital delay with harmonizer. Eventide Flanger. Four DBX 120 compressors. Four gain brains. Twelve Kepex.
Two LA 1176's. Two LA 3A leveling amplifiers. One URE graphic equalizer.

Thermostatically controlled echo chamber. Disc to tape facilities.

A Pictorial History

Ringo O' Records

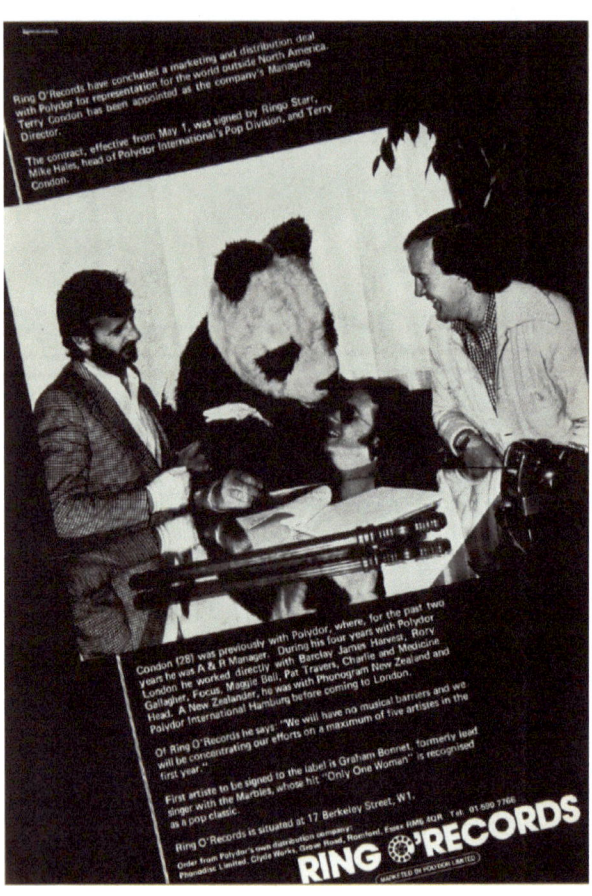

On April 4, 1975, Ringo officially declared that RING O' RECORDS was ready to sign artists and produce records. Ringo, Ringo was not an active participant in the company, nor was he signed to the label. Over a three-year period, more than half a dozens albums, and over a dozen singles were released. In North America, Capitol Records distributed the first two singles and the first album. After a brief hiatus, in the Spring of 1977 Polydor became the worldwide distributor for the newly re-launched RING O' RECORDS. Less than a dozen musical artists recorded for the label.

David Hentschel
Startling Music
Release date: 1975
Instrumental version of Ringo Starr's album 'Ringo'.
Credits: David Hentschel - producer, arranger, musician, engineer
Recorded and mixed at Startling Studios, Ascot, England

Tittenhurst Park

A Pictorial History

In 1984 David Tickle returned to Tittenhurst Park, this time as the producer of the second studio album by Canadian musician Lawrence Gowan, entitled Strange Animal. The album would go on to reach #5 on the Canadian album charts and spawned the singles "(You're a) Strange Animal", "A Criminal Mind", "Cosmetics" and "Guerilla Soldier".

Tittenhurst Park

Soon after David Tickle scheduled to produce the album and arrange the recording sessions he hired several session musicians, including bassist Tony Levin, drummer Jerry Marotta, and guitarist David Rhodes, all of whom had been a part of the backing band for Peter Gabriel. (Gowan collection)

> The studio's in the house, just off the kitchen and about halfway through making the record, Ringo had popped in because he was living there at the time, and he would come in the studio occasionally and make a comment or two. And one day "Cosmetics" was playing and he came through the kitchen door, he had a big smile on his face and he said to me, [imitates Ringo's voice] "We love it every time this song comes on 'cause we all start dancing around the kit when we hear this one start up." - Gowan.

A Pictorial History

Zayed bin Sultan Al Nahyan

In 1988 Ringo Starr sold the property for £5 million to Sheikh Zayed bin Sultan Al Nahyan, President of the United Arab Emirates and ruler of Abu Dhabi.

Tittenhurst Park

Zayed bin Sultan Al Nahyan (May 6, 1918 – Nov. 2, 2004) was the principal driving force behind the formation of the United Arab Emirates (UAE), the Ruler of Abu Dhabi and first President of the UAE, a post which he held for a period of over 33 years (1971–2004). His father was the ruler of Abu Dhabi from 1922 until his assassination in 1926. Zayed was named after his grandfather, Sheikh Zayed bin Khalifa Al Nahyan ("Zayed the Great"), who ruled the emirate from 1855 to 1909. Zayed was considered one of the wealthiest men in the world. A Forbes estimate put his fortune at around US$20 billion. The source of this wealth could be attributed to the immense oil wealth of Abu Dhabi and the Emirates, which sit on a pool of a tenth of the world's proven oil reserves. Using the country's enormous oil revenues, Zayed built institutions such as hospitals, schools and universities and made it possible for UAE citizens to enjoy free access to them. Other charitable acts included adopting hundreds of orphans and building several hospitals abroad in Europe, Asia, and Africa. In 1988, he purchased, for £5m, Tittenhurst Park at Sunninghill, Berkshire as his English home

A Pictorial History

During Zayed's renovations of Tittenhurst in 1989 and 1990, the walls of the house were gutted, reinforced, and rebuilt. The east-side porch was enclosed in glass. The portion of the house where Lennon once had his studio was widened, and a 2nd floor was added. The Temple was enlarged, including the basement where staff now live. The terrace cottages were also enlarged, as were the garages and lodge house. Another structure, matching the gate lodge, was built on the other side of the entry gate.

The firm of Charles Funke Associates was hired to restore and transform the parkland, arboretum, waterbodies and formal gardens. The team was hire to design major new water courses, earthworks and prepare planting schemes throughout the site.

Tittenhurst Park

Where there was once open field with a handful of trees was created a unique circular-shaped garden divided and encircled by a strem valley & waterway, and bespeckled with carefully maintained trees and breeden gravel paths.

A Pictorial History

Tittenhurst Today

View of Tittenhurst Park from above c. 2017 offers unique glimpse of the enormous size of the estate beginning with the garage complex on the top left, extending to the strucutres on the right that were once part of the stables, gardener's buildings, and agricultural land, and down to the circular-shaped garden at the southern end.

View of Tittenhurst Park from above c. 2017. This angle offers a rare glimpse of the extraordinary property and spectacular "museum of trees" throughout the landscape. (DavidGoddard.com collection)

A Pictorial History

Notes & References

p. 8, 9, 12, 13, 16. Tittenhurst Park Wikipedia, Williams, Richard (1983). "Royal Holloway College, A Pictorial History" (first published October 1983). Surrey: Royal Holloway, University of London. pp. 6 – includes a picture of the house ca. 1930. ISBN 0-900145-83-8., Historic England, "Tittenhurst (1109930)", National Heritage List for England,

p. 10. 11. Sunningdale Wikipedia, "Civil Parish population 2011". Neighbourhood Statistics. Office for National Statistics., Royal Borough of Windsor & Maidenhead: Sunningdale.

p. 12, 13. Thomas Holloway Wikipedia, History of Royal Holloway and Bedford New College, RootsWeb.com's page on Thomas Holloway.

p. 14. Holloway Sanatorium Wikipedia, Papers of George Martin-Holloway Royal Holloway, University of London Archives, An institution, not an asylum or hospital.

p.15. Royal Holloway, University of London (Wikipedia), Bingham, Caroline (1987). The history of the Royal Holloway College 1886–1986. London: Constable. ISBN 0-09-468200-3.

p. 17. Sothebys.com/fr/auctions/ecatalogue/2009/american-paintings-drawings-sculpture-n08555/lot.79, Harvard Art Museums.

p. 18, 19. Peter Cadbury (Wikipedia), Martin Adeney. "Obituary: Peter Cadbury | Media". The Guardian..

p. 20, 21. John Lennon Wikipedia, Norman, Philip (2008). John Lennon: The Life. Hammersmith, England: Harper Collins. pp. 615 et seq., Blaney, John (2005). John Lennon: Listen To This Book. Guildford, Great Britain: Biddles Ltd. p. 89.

p. 22, 23. Daniel Richter (actor) Wikipedia, The Dream is Over by Dan Richter, page 149. *The Fool were a Dutch design collective and band in the psychedelic style of art in British popular music in the late 1960s. The group was named in reference to the Fool tarot card.

p. 25. Tittenhurst Park Wiki, Ringo Star Wiki, Maureen Starkey Tigrett Wiki.

p. 78-81, Debs Skeldon Imagine there is a Studio article.

p. 93. Zayed bin Sultan Al Nahyan Wiki.

(opposite, right) East lawn, showing 90+ ft. tall Incense Cedar and house in the distance. (Peter Blakey collection)

A Pictorial History

www.ingramcontent.com/pod-product-compliance
Lightning Source LLC
Chambersburg PA
CBHW042314150426
43200CB00004B/38